Best Bler

Recipe Book

Simple, Versatile Blender Recipes

BY

Rachael Rayner

Copyright 2019 Rachael Rayner

License Notes

No part of this Book can be reproduced in any form or by any means including print, electronic, scanning or photocopying unless prior permission is granted by the author.

All ideas, suggestions and guidelines mentioned here are written for informative purposes. While the author has taken every possible step to ensure accuracy, all readers are advised to follow information at their own risk. The author cannot be held responsible for personal and/or commercial damages in case of misinterpreting and misunderstanding any part of this Book

Table of Contents

Introduction 6

    What Can You Do with A Blender? 8

    How Does A Blender Work? 10

    Difference Between A Blender and A Food Processor 14

    How To Clean A Blender 18

Blender Recipes 20

    Blender Hollandaise Sauce 21

    Clean Coconut Protein Shake 24

    Starbucks Caramel Frappuccino Copycat Recipe 26

    Banana Split Workout Protein Smoothie 28

    Blueberry Smoothie 31

    Mango Lassi Smoothie 34

    Watermelon Cooler Slushy 37

    Chia Seed Berry Yoghurt Smoothie 40

Pineapple and Banana Smoothie 43

Kale and Orange Smoothie 45

Green Slime Smoothie 47

No-Bake Oatmeal Chocolate Chip Energy Bites 50

Filipino Avocado Milkshake 54

Fruit Energy Bars 57

Cinnapear Smoothie 60

Beet Coconut Water Detox 63

Chocolate-Banana Tofu Pudding 65

Vitamin Boost Detox Juice 68

Carrot-Ginger Dressing 71

Avocado Hummus 74

Pumpkin Pie Smoothie 77

Creamy Avocado and Spinach Dip 80

White Bean Hummus 83

Eggless Mayonaise 86

Lemon Frozen Yogurt 89

Chocolate Peanut Butter Banana Ice Cream 92

Spinach Ice Cream 95

Skinny Watermelon Sorbet 98

Dill Dip 100

Butternut Squash Soup 103

Conclusion 106

Author's Afterthoughts 107

About the Author 108

Introduction

A blender, also known as a liquidizer seems like a simple tool, and for the most part, it is. It is among the essential kitchen appliance that is used to mix, puree, or emulsify varieties of foods including soft raw fruits, cooked foods, and vegetables including tomatoes, onions, mushrooms, and peppers. This is done by a set of basic blending functions to help you achieve the consistency you need for a certain recipe.

Some powerful models are used in homes and bars to crush ice. These are designed with a stainless blade for this purpose. If you're not sure what to use, the pulse setting is enough and appropriate for many blending tasks. Models that have a variety of functions are relatively high-powered, features additional chopping tools, and are a bit pricey for that matter.

Although different blenders have a set of different features and functions, many blenders, even the cheaper ones, are useful for meeting your kitchen needs. The key features you may want to look out for when shopping for a blender are:

- Ease of use
- Visible measurement characters
- Low noise when in use
- Low power usage (preferably between 300 and 1000 watts)
- Sufficient pulse blending
- Ease of cleaning

What Can You Do with A Blender?

Even if you don't plan to use a blender for cooking, it is no doubt a handy appliance to have in your kitchen. When you want to prepare fruit smoothies or homemade milkshakes, a blend is a go-to tool.

The obvious is, blenders seem to perform the same task. Though true, there are different types of blenders, and each model offers extraordinary features to help achieve customer needs. The most common types of blenders in the market include conventional, immersion, multi-purpose, and personal.

A conventional blender is the most popular type that can be found in most homes. It can be used to blend smoothies and prepare the soup. The immersion blenders, also called hands blenders are famous alternatives to other blenders and can be used with any container. Multi-function blenders are the high-end types that are common in restaurants and bars.

Finally, we have the personal blender, which is a bit smaller than the rest and used to make single servings. Because of the portability nature, they can run from a battery.

How Does A Blender Work?

Will it blend? Yes, any time, if you get the right blender in your kitchen.

Due to their exceptionally high power and speed, blenders have raised eyeballs on exactly how they work. The power and speed require a lot of attention, but the rest is not difficult to connect the dots and understand how a blender motor works.

The main features to look out for to understand the difference between the different types of blenders are moto speed, design, and controls.

Motor Speed

As is the case with most electric motors, a blender motors speed is indicated in watts. Most of the household blender models fall within the range of 500 to 750 watts, but they can go as high as 1500 watts depending on the model. The high wattage models are often expensive than their low watt counterparts.

Although these blenders can run at high speeds, they are not designed to sustain such speed for too long as it can heat the motor faster which can damage the blender. To avoid any potential damage, make sure you regulate the speed of your blender to ensure speeds are produced in short intervals, instead of continuous higher speeds.

Controls

Blender controls are different depending on the model. A typical blender may have three-speed features (low, medium, and high) but a good number offer seven or more speeds. This provides a wide array of options whether to chop, mix, puree, or liquefy. Some go an extra mile with functions that suggest speeds for sauces, juices, or milkshakes.

In addition to controls, the jar is a key feature in every blender. Majority of blender jars are made of three materials including glass, stainless steel, and polycarbonate. Which one to use depends on your personal preferences. Glass materials are delicate, but they are heavy which makes them more stable.

They are also resistant to scratch and odors. Stainless steel is sleek and more elegant, which makes them extremely attractive, but it's hard to see inside, so you might be forced to stop the blender to see if the content has liquefied. Polycarbonate jars are slightly light and hard to shatter in case the blender drops on the floor; however, they are likely to get scratches and may end up having unpleasant odors.

When blending, first fill your blender with the liquid ingredients, followed by the rest of the content. If you're using hot liquids, ensure you blend them carefully and start from low speed all the way up.

Design:

When it comes to design, blenders have experienced tremendous changes in the last ten decades. Currently, the designs range from no-frills to modern styles to retro. Simply, there are many options to cater to your needs. Be sure to do your research before settling on the actual design you're looking for.

Difference Between A Blender and A Food Processor

With all the kitchen appliances available in the market, it can be hard to identify the difference and what works for you. But all these appliances are not created equal. Some may have pretty similar features, but there is a difference that should make the process of choosing quite simple.

A blender and a food processor are perfect examples that may look similar, but they have a striking difference.

The Shape: Blenders features a rotating blade that is cone-shaped at the base to ensure content falls naturally towards the center of the jug. Food processors, on the other hand, are huge, flat bowls, with two blades bearing different heights. They are designed for crushing solid food into finer pieces.

Functions: Both kitchen appliances can be used to mix ingredients, but the difference is the shape of the base that specifies the purpose for which it is designed.

A blender is primarily used to prepare soup, smoothies, dips, sauces, and cocktails. A food processor comes with a flat base, making it ideal for performing multiple functions, such as grating, chopping, pureeing, slicing, making nut butter, and kneading dough if you need it for bread or pastry.

Accessories: Majority of blenders feature only one set of blades and a jug. Although some may include extra jugs for dry food, for most there's just one set. Food processors, often feature a variety of accessories, such as graters, slicers, dough blades, and many more.

Price: A food processor is slightly expensive compared to a blender. But, both of these kitchen appliances fall in a similar price range. Jug blenders may range from as low as $20 up to $600, while food processors fall between $40 and $800.

The Best Foods to Blend and Not to Blend

Wondering which food to and not to blend in a jug blender, this list should clear those doubts

The best foods to blend

You can use a standard jar blender to prepare a variety of foods and recipes. You can blend soup and gravy, puree soft or cooked foods, frozen juices, eggs, eggnog, creampie, custards, smoothies, homemade pancake, salad dressings, ice cream shakes, dips, puddings, bread, salsas, cracker, mayonnaise, and crush ice as well as blend frozen beverages.

Foods not to blend

If you have no idea what a blender can or cannot do, always refer to your product manual, as capabilities often vary depending on the model. If you want more than just a simple puree, you can get one or two recipe books to bring out the potential of your blender.

That said, you should never use a blender to whip egg white, mash potatoes, extract juice from fruits and vegetables, knead the dough, grind raw meats, or blend dry or hard vegetables.

How To Clean A Blender

If you love purees, smoothies, or juices, that means your blender is in use every day. But how do you clean it?

Cleaning a blender shouldn't be a hard task, but it involves more than scrubbing a saucepan or tossing any appliance in the dishwater.

To make cleaning of a blender easier, you need a sponge or dishrag, mild dish soap or baking soda.

Take the blender apart. Unplug the unit and remove the jar from the motor base. Then unscrew the base and remove the jar lid.

Pour a small amount of warm water and soap in the jar, about halfway.

Clean the jar using a sponge or dish rage then rinse thoroughly and dry it carefully.

Go ahead and clean the other small parts including the cutting blade, gasket seal, and jar base. Rinse these parts thoroughly and leave them to dry.

Remember, never submerge the base of the jar in water. Once you're done, reassemble the jar and store it in a safe location where you can access it easily.

Blender Recipes

Blender Hollandaise Sauce

Using a blender is the coolest way to obtain a perfect hollandaise sauce. This recipe uses the same ingredient as the classic recipe with no gamble of sauce separation. It has a lemony flavor that you will love and enjoy.

Time: 10 Minutes | **Servings:** 1

Ingredients

- 3 egg yolks
- 1/4 tbsp Dijon mustard
- 1tbsp lemon juice
- 1 pepper sauce (hot)
- 1/2 Cup butter

Method

Place egg yolks, pepper sauce, lemon juice and mustard in a blender container then cover and blend for about 5 seconds.

Heat butter placed in a glass measuring cup in a microwave for about 1 minute. Heat until hot and melted.

Set blender to high then add butter to the egg mixture in a stream (thin). The mixture should immediately thicken.

Place the container with the mixture on a pan with hot tap water for 1 minute.

Serve and enjoy.

Nutritional Information

Calories: 163

Fat: 17.5g

Carbs: 0.6g

Protein: 1.5g

Cholesterol: 143mg

Sodium: 119mg

Clean Coconut Protein Shake

Are you looking for a recovery meal after your workout, a great breakfast to kick off your day with or an awesome snack for your sweet cravings? This coconut protein shake is an ideal blender recipe for you. You need not miss it on your list.

Time: 10 Minutes | **Serving:** 1 ½ Cups

Ingredients

- 1 2/3 coconut milk (chilled)
- 1 cup baby spinach
- 1 banana (frozen and pre-sliced)
- 2 scoops protein powder (clean vanilla)

Method

Add all the ingredients in a blender and blend until creamy and smooth.

Add ice if you desire a thick shake. Serve and enjoy.

Nutritional Information

Cal: 204

Fat: 12g

Carbs: 17g

Fiber: 2g

Protein: 15g

Sugar: 11g

Starbucks Caramel Frappuccino Copycat Recipe

This is a health blender recipe to include in your diet plan. Coffee is a rich source of caffeine which can increase levels of adrenaline and facilitates the release of fatty acids from the fat tissues.

Time: 20 Minutes | **Servings:** 2

Ingredients

- 2 Cups ice
- 1 cup cooled brewed coffee (strong)
- 1 cup milk (low-fat)
- 1/3 cup caramel sauce
- 3tbsp white sugar

Method

Put coffee, ice, sugar, milk and caramel sauce in a blender. Blend on high speed until smooth.

Divide between two 16-ounces glasses and serve.

Nutritional Information

Calories: 271

Fat: 2.5g

Carbs: 60.2g

Protein: 5g

Cholesterol: 10mg

Sodium: 249mg

Banana Split Workout Protein Smoothie

Who doesn't enjoy banana split flavor? This workout protein smoothie powers you up in an awesome way after working out. Take it for breakfast to awesomely start your day. Preparing this blender recipe is easy.

Time: 20 Minutes | **Servings:** 1

Ingredients

- 1 tbsp dark cocoa powder (unsweetened)
- 1 tbsp chocolate protein powder
- 1 banana
- 1/4 Cup strawberries (fresh and diced)
- 1 tbsp peanut butter (natural)
- 1/4 Cup coconut milk
- Ice

Method

Put all the Ingredients in a blender and blend until smooth. Add coconut milk until the desired consistency is achieved.

Frozen berries may be used instead of ice for a cold smoothie.

Nutritional Information

Cal: 346

Fat: 17g

Carbs: 39g

Fiber: 7g

Protein: 14g

Sugar: 21g

Blueberry Smoothie

This is one of the most delicious blueberry blender recipes to include in your recipe book. Blueberry juice, in several studies, helps in the reduction of DNA damage, thereby preventing aging and cancer.

Time: 10 Minutes | **Servings:** 1

Ingredients

- 1 cup fresh blueberries
- 1 container (8-ounces) plain yogurt
- 3/4 cup milk (2% reduced fat)
- 2tbsp white sugar
- 1/2 tbsp vanilla extract
- 1/8 tbsp nutmeg (ground)

Method

Place yogurt, milk, blueberries, nutmeg, vanilla and sugar in a blender.

Blend until foamy. Use a spatula occasionally to scrap down blender sides.

Serve immediately and enjoy.

Nutritional Information

Calories: 211

Fat: 3.9g

Carbs: 35.5g

Protein: 9.5g

Cholesterol: 14mg

Sodium: 118mg

Mango Lassi Smoothie

This Indian tradition mango lassi smoothie is perfect cool-down drink in summer or on a hot afternoon. This creamy and refreshingly tangy blender recipe is worth a place in your recipe book.

Time: 10 Minutes | **Serving:** 2

Ingredients

- 1 cup mango (cut into pieces)
- 1 1/2 cup Greek yogurt
- 1/4 tbsp cinnamon
- 1/(8) tbsp cardamom (ground)
- 1/4 Cup milk (coconut, dairy, almond, soy)
- 1 tbsp honey (raw)
- 3 ice cubes

Method

Place all the Ingredients in your blender and blend until very smooth.

In case of leftover smoothie, put in a freezer up to a week. Enjoy.

Nutritional Information

Cal: 213

Fat: 3g

Carbs: 38g

Fiber: 1g

Protein: 10g

Sugar: 37g

Watermelon Cooler Slushy

This is the best blender recipe for the hot summer days. Watermelon has high contents of water that best for summer to keep the body hydrated and keeping you full.

Time: 20 Minutes | **Servings:** 1

Ingredients

- 4 Cups watermelon (seedless and cubed)
- 10 ice cubes
- 1/3 cup lime juice (fresh)
- 1/4 cup white sugar
- 1/8 tbsp salt

Method

Place ice cubes and watermelon in a blender. Add sugar, lime juice, and salt.

Blend until becomes smooth.

Serve.

Nutritional Information

Calories: 79

Fat: 0.2g

Carbs: 20.6g

Protein: 0.8g

Cholesterol: 0mg

Sodium: 61mg

Chia Seed Berry Yoghurt Smoothie

Are you looking for a balanced breakfast to start your day with? This chia seed berry yogurt smoothie is rich in protein keeping you full for a long time. This blender recipe is also a perfect after-workout energy boost.

Time: Minutes | **Servings:** 1

Ingredients

- 1 cup orange juice (no sugar)
- 2 tbsp chia seeds
- 1/2 Cup strawberries (fresh)
- 1/2 Cup blueberries (fresh)
- 1/2 Cup raspberries (fresh)
- 1/2 Cup blackberries (fresh)
- 1 banana (cut in quarters)
- 2 tbsp honey
- 1/4 tbsp cinnamon
- 2 Cups Greek yogurt (plain)

Method

In a mixing bowl, thoroughly mix orange juice and chia seeds then refrigerate. The juice absorbs the seeds, and the mixture becomes gel-like.

Meanwhile, add all the other ingredients in a blender and blend until smooth.

Add the gel to the blender and continue blending until well combined.

Serve and enjoy.

Nutritional Information

Cal: 277

Fat: 10g

Carbs: 38g

Fiber: 6g

Protein: 13g

Sugar: 27g

Pineapple and Banana Smoothie

This is a healthy blender recipe making an indulgent and gorgeous smoothie. Pineapple makes the smoothie healthy since it's a rich source of antioxidants which helps to reduce risks of some chronic diseases like diabetes, heart diseases, and other cancer types.

Time: 6 Minutes | **Servings:** 1

Ingredients

- 4 ice cubes
- 1/4 fresh pineapple (peeled, cubed and cored)
- 1 banana (large and cut to chunks)
- 1 cup pineapple juice

Method

Place all the ingredients in a blender container.

Blend on high until smooth.

Serve.

Nutritional Information

Calories: 313

Fat: 0.9g

Carbs: 78.7g

Protein: 3g

Cholesterol: 0mg

Sodium: 10mg

Kale and Orange Smoothie

This sweet kale, orange smoothie is loaded with minerals and vitamins definitely worth a trial when you are craving sweetness and want to keep it healthy. This blender recipe fits in your easy recipe book.

Time: 10 Minutes | **Servings:** 2

Ingredients

- 1 banana (peeled, chopped and frozen)
- 1 cup kale leaves (loosely packed)
- 1 orange (peeled)
- 2 tbsp honey (raw)
- 2 Cups almond milk

Method

Add all the ingredients in a blender then blend until smooth.

Add ice cubes for a cool smoothie. Serve and enjoy.

Nutritional Information

Cal: 127

Fat: 0g

Carbs: 23g

Fiber: 7g

Protein: 4g

Sugar: 12g

Green Slime Smoothie

This is a yummy blender recipe that the kids will love. Spinach is an excellent and good source of iron. Iron helps in the creation of hemoglobin which transports oxygen to body tissues. Besides, strawberries are rich in vitamin c, iodine, and phytochemicals that help in maintaining a properly working of the nervous system.

Time: 1 Hour 10 Minutes | **Servings:** 4

Ingredients

- 2 Cups spinach
- 2 Cups strawberries (frozen)
- 1 banana
- 2tbsp honey
- 1/2 cup ice

Method

Freeze the spinach for about 1 hour in a freezer.

Place the spinach, banana, strawberries, honey, and ice in a blender then blend on high until smooth.

Immediately serve.

Nutritional Information

Calories: 100

Fat: 0.3g

Carbs: 26g

Protein: 1.3g

Cholesterol: 0mg

Sodium: 16mg

No-Bake Oatmeal Chocolate Chip Energy Bites

Are there times when you feel like your energy is flagging and need a quick boost? Then these chocolate chip energy bites are the best for you.

Time: 30 Minutes | **Servings:** 20 Energy Bites

Ingredients

- 2 1/4 Cups oats
- 3 tbsp chia seeds
- 1tbsp cocoa powder
- 1/4 Cup unsweetened coconut (shredded)
- 1/8 tbsp salt
- 1 ripe banana
- 1 cup almond or peanut butter (smooth)
- 1/3 Cup honey (raw)
- 1 tbsp real vanilla extract
- 1/2 Cup chocolate chips (bittersweet or dark)

Method

Line a wax paper (square) on a sealable container.

Use your blender to grind a quarter cup of oats until you obtain flour-like consistency.

Pour the oats flour in a large mixing bowl, followed by the remained oats. Add chia seeds, cocoa powder, coconut, and salt then mix until well combined.

Blend the banana or use a fork to puree the banana. Add the banana, butter, honey, and vanilla extract; chocolate then mix until well mixed.

Use your hands to make twenty balls placing them on the lined wax paper. Place another square wax paper on the bites to make another layer of bites. Make the bites until all the mixture is done.

Place the bites on your fridge to refrigerate

Nutritional Information

Cal: 203

Fat: 11g

Carbs: 24g

Fiber: 4g

Protein: 6g

Sugar: 8g

Filipino Avocado Milkshake

This is a rich, stupendous, refreshing and creamy blender recipe to have in your diet plan. Avocados are a good source of fiber and are very low in carbohydrates which promote weight loss.

Time: 10 Minutes | **Servings:** 2

Ingredients

- 1 peeled and cubed avocado (pitted)
- 5 ice cubes
- 3tbsp white sugar
- 1 1/3 Cups milk
- 1tbsp lime juice
- 1 scoop ice cream (vanilla)

Method

Place all the Ingredients in a blender.

Blend until smooth.

Serve immediately and enjoy.

Nutritional Information

Calories: 336

Fat: 19.1g

Carbs: 37.6g

Protein: 7.8g

Cholesterol: 18mg

Sodium: 84mg

Fruit Energy Bars

This fruit energy bar is an amazing blender recipe to add in your diet plan. These fantastic energy bars are tasty and can be carried in your bag to kill that craving in the summer months.

Time: 30 Minutes | **Servings:** 8 BARS

Ingredients

- 1– 1/2 Cups Medjool dates (pitted)
- 1/2 Cup apricots
- 1/(2) Cups almonds
- 3 tbsp chia seeds
- 3 tbsp water
- 2 tbsp sunflower seeds (hulled)
- 2 tbsp cocoa powder (unsweetened)
- 1 tbsp flax seeds
- 1tbsp orange juice
- 1/4 tbsp cinnamon
- 1/8 tbsp salt

Method

Put all the ingredients in your blender and blend while occasionally stopping to scrape the sides using a spatula.

Check if the mixture can ball up and if not add little water at a time until it balls up.

Place the mixture on a wax paper sheet and form a ball. Refrigerate overnight.

Remove from fridge and flatten into a square between two wax paper sheets. Cut into bars and enjoy.

Nutritional Information

Cal: 209

Fat: 6g

Carbs: 41g

Fiber: 6g

Protein: 4g

Sugar: 33g

Cinnapear Smoothie

This is a combination of pears and cinnamon that you will absolutely love. It is a very charming drink for breakfast when tossed in milk, banana and other few things. Frozen banana makes it even more refreshing.

Time: 20 Minutes | **Servings:** 2

Ingredients

- 2 quartered pears (cores removed)
- 1 chunk cut banana
- 1 cup milk
- 1/2 cup vanilla yogurt
- 1/2 tbsp cinnamon (ground)
- 1 pinch nutmeg (ground)

Method

Place pears, milk, yogurt, banana, nutmeg, and cinnamon in a blender and blend until smooth,

Divide into two glasses to serve.

Enjoy!

Nutritional Information

Calories: 266

Fat: 3.8g

Carbs: 54g

Protein: 8.4g

Cholesterol: 13mg

Sodium: 93mg

Beet Coconut Water Detox

Not only is this homemade blender recipe detox healthy, but it also tastes yummy. This beet coconut water detox cleanses your vital body organs flushing out toxins from your body. This recipe is worth a place in your recipe book.

Time: 10 Minutes | **Servings:** 1

Ingredients

- 1 beet (medium-sized, peeled and chopped coarsely)
- 2 Cups coconut water (chilled with no sugar added)
- 1 lemon juice

Method

Place all the ingredients in a blender and blend until beets turn into juice.

Pour into a glass and place one slice of the lemon on the glass edge. Enjoy.

Nutritional Information

Cal: 143

Fat: 1g

Carbs: 31g

Fiber: 5g

Protein: 5g

Sugar: 20g

Chocolate-Banana Tofu Pudding

This blender recipe is lovely, guilt-free and only takes just 5 Minutes to be ready. It is best for everyone including the kids. Cocoa contains flavanols that improve the flow of blood to the skin thus protecting the skin from sun harm.

Time: 1 HOUR 20 Minutes | **Servings:** 4

Ingredients

- 1 chunk cut banana
- 1 soft silken tofu (12-ounce package)
- 1/4 cup sugar (confectioners'
- 5tbsp cocoa powder
- 3tbsp soy milk
- 1 pinch cinnamon (ground)

Method

Place banana, cocoa powder, tofu, soy milk, sugar and cinnamon in a blender.

Cover the blender and blend until smooth.

Divide among four individual dishes.

Refrigerate for about 1 hour then serve.

Nutritional Information

Calories: 124

Fat: 3.5g

Carbs: 21.2g

Protein: 6.1g

Cholesterol: 0mg

Sodium: 12mg

Vitamin Boost Detox Juice

How do you cleanse your body when you need to detox? This mixture of veggies and fruits is great in both health and flavor. It's extremely easy to prepare since a blender is all that is needed to put it together.

Time: 10 Minutes | **Servings:** 2

Ingredients

- 1 carrot (chopped)
- 1 orange (peeled)
- 1 green apple (chopped after being seeded)
- 3 kale leaves
- 1 cup baby spinach
- 1/(2) Lemon (peeled)
- 1/(4) tbsp ginger

Method

Add the ingredients in a blender, two Cups of chilled water and blend until they are smooth.

Alternatively, place all the ingredients in your juicer and juice. Enjoy.

Nutritional Information

Cal: 116

Fat: 1g

Carbs: 27g

Fiber: 7g

Protein: 3g

Sugar: 17g

Carrot-Ginger Dressing

This is one of the easiest lunch blender recipes to have. Carrots are a rich source of vitamin A which helps in the promotion of good vision, immune function, development and important for body growth.

Time: | **Servings:** 1

Ingredients

- 4 roughly chopped carrots (medium)
- 1 roughly chopped fresh ginger (1-inch)
- 1 sliced shallot
- 3 tbsp rice vinegar
- 1 tbsp sesame oil
- 1 tbsp soy sauce
- 1/4 cup vegetable oil

Method

Put all ingredients in a blender and blend on high until chopped finely.

Add vegetable oil slowly then continue to blend till smooth.

Add water if needed to make it thin

Refrigerate for up to one week in an airtight container.

Nutritional Information

Calories: 195

Fat: 17.6g

Carbs: 9.1g

Fiber: 2.3g

Sugars: 4.1g

Protein: 1.1g

Sodium: 117.4mg

Avocado Hummus

Avocado hummus is a no-effort dish that requires you to just add all the **Ingredients** in blender and blend. Add this avocado hummus into your snacks diet plan and enjoy it at any time of the day. Accompany this hummus with whole grain pita chips.

Time: 15 Minutes | **Servings:** 8

Ingredients

- 1 avocado (ripe, peeled and pitted)
- 15 Oz can garbanzo beans (drained and rinsed)
- 2 tbsp tahini
- 1/(2) tbsp salt
- 3 tbsp lime juice (fresh and squeezed)
- 2 garlic cloves (minced)
- 2 tbsp virgin olive oil

Method

Add all the Ingredients in a blender.

Blend until smooth. Add water for a thinner consistency is desired.

Serve and enjoy.

Nutritional Information

Cal: 168

Fat: 10g

Carbs: 16g

Fiber: 5g

Protein: 5g

Sugar: 2g

Pumpkin Pie Smoothie

This is one of the easiest blender recipes to have on your recipe book. It is a healthy recipe since pumpkins are a rich source of vitamin C which increases production of white blood cells making wounds to heal faster and helping immune cells to work more efficiently.

Time: 40 Seconds | **Servings:** 4

Ingredients

- 1/2 cup apple juice
- 1 cup vanilla yogurt (fat-free)
- 1 cup ice cubes
- 1/2 peeled orange
- 1tbsp pie spice pumpkin
- 1 cup pumpkin puree

Method

Add all the ingredients in a blender (wildside+ jar) in the listed order.

Cover the blender and blend for 40 seconds.

Enjoy!

Nutritional Information

calories: 84

Fat: 0g

Cholesterol: 1mg

Sodium: 40mg

Carbs: 19g

Fiber: 2g

Sugar: 13g

Protein: 3g

Creamy Avocado and Spinach Dip

This blender recipe is a combination of two super healthy foods: spinach and avocado. This avocado and spinach dip is the best idea for guacamole fans. It's creamy and amazingly delicious.

Time: 5 Minutes | **Servings:** 12

Ingredients

- 1 avocado (peeled and pitted)
- 1 cup baby spinach (loosely packed)
- 1 garlic clove
- 1/(3) Cup red onion (chopped and diced)
- 1 cup clean mayo
- 1 tbsp lime juice (freshly squeezed)
- 1/4 tbsp red pepper flakes (crushed)
- 1/(4) tbsp salt
- 1/(4) tbsp black pepper

Method

Put all the ingredients in a blender and blend until smooth.

Add the dip to a container then refrigerate overnight.

Serve with veggies of your choice. Enjoy.

Nutritional Information

Cal: 164

Fat: 13g

Carbs: 10g

Fiber: 5g

Protein: 4g

Sugar: 3g

White Bean Hummus

This is a healthy and delicious blender recipe to have. White beans contain dietary fiber which helps in fighting cancer. Eating white beans reduces cancer risks and any potential killer, brain aneurysms included.

Time: 25 SECONDS | **Servings:** 6

Ingredients

- 2tbsp olive oil
- 2tbsp lemon juice
- 2tbsp tahini
- 2 garlic cloves
- 1/2 tbsp salt
- 1 (15 0z. can) drained white beans
- 1/2 tbsp cumin (ground)
- 2 drops Tabasco sauce

Method

Add all Ingredients in the listed order to a blender (wildside+ jar).

Blend for about 25 seconds on medium-low speed.

Serve.

Nutritional Information

Calories: 150

Fat: 7g

Cholesterol: 0mg

Sodium: 200mg

Carbs: 16g

Fiber: 3g

Sugar: 0g

Protein: 6g

Eggless Mayonaise

This blender eggless mayo is a must in the summer time. It's awesome and tangy in salads and on sandwiches. It's easy and fast to prepare so include it in your quick diet plan. Feel free to add spices and herbs of your choice.

Time: 40 Minutes| **Servings:** 3/4 cup

Ingredients

- 1/4 Cup milk (unsweetened)
- 1 tbsp mustard powder
- 1 tbsp organic sugar
- 1/2 tbsp white vinegar (mild)
- 1/2 tbsp lemon juice
- 1/4 tbsp sea salt
- Pinch of paprika
- 1/2 Cup canola oil

Method

Put all the Ingredients in a blender except the oil. Purse until a slightly creamy consistency is achieved.

Add oil and continue to blend until the mixture has mayonnaise consistency.

Put in a fridge for about an hour.

Serve and enjoy.

Nutritional Information

Cal: 122

Fat: 11g

Carbs: 6g

Fiber: 3g

Protein: 2g

Sugar: 2g

Lemon Frozen Yogurt

This is a blender recipe that you will love since it offers entire golly with no guilt. Lemons are a good source of vitamin C which reduces skin wrinkling, damage from sun and aging of dry skin.

Time: 45 Seconds | **Servings:** 8

Ingredients

- 1/3 cup lemon juice (fresh)
- 1 1/2 Cups vanilla yogurt (whole-fat)
- 2tbsp agave nectar
- 1/2 banana
- 4 Cups ice cubes

Method

Add all Ingredients in the listed order to a blender (wildside+ jar).

Cover the blender and blend for 15 seconds on low-speed then 30 seconds on medium-high speed.

Serve and enjoy.

Nutritional Information

Calories: 72

Fat: 1g

Cholesterol: 6mg

Sodium: 25mg

Carbs: 13g

Fiber: 1g

Sugar: 11g

Protein: 1g

Chocolate Peanut Butter Banana Ice Cream

Let's all face it, who doesn't love enjoying ice cream at the end of the tiresome and hot day? This peanut butter banana ice cream is the answer to healthily satisfying those ice cream cravings.

Time: 20 Minutes | **Servings:** 3

Ingredients

- 2 frozen bananas (ripe, peeled, and sliced)
- 1 cup greek yogurt (plain)
- 1 tbsp honey (pure)
- 2 tbsp peanut butter
- 1 tbsp cocoa powder (unsweetened)
- Strawberries (fresh and sliced) for topping
- Peanuts (chopped)

Method

Put all the Ingredients in a blender except strawberries and peanuts and blend until very smooth.

Top with strawberries and peanuts. Enjoy.

Nutritional Information

Cal: 241

Fat: 11g

Carbs: 30g

Fiber: 3g

Protein: 11g

Sugar: 20g

Spinach Ice Cream

This blender recipe is delicious, sweet. Almond flavored crammed with green produce IS low in calories. Everyone will love the spinach ice cream and feel good eating it.

Time: 45 Seconds | **Servings:** 7

Ingredients

- 2fl.oz agave nectar
- 6fl.oz almond milk
- 1tbsp almond extract
- 1oz. avocado
- 3 1/2 Cups ice cubes
- 3 Cups spinach
- 1/4cup whey protein powder (vanilla)

Method

Place all Ingredients in a blender (wildside+ jar).

Cover and blend for about 40 seconds on medium-low speed.

Serve immediately.

Nutritional Information

Calories: 75

Fat: 2g

Cholesterol: 0mg

Sodium: 51mg

Carbs: 11g

Fiber: 1g

Sugar: 9g

Protein: 3g

Skinny Watermelon Sorbet

Creamy? Check. Easy to prepare? Check. Sweet? Check. This watermelon sorbet is an awesomely delicious dessert, low in calories and packed with **Ingredients** meeting all your diet requirements.

Time: 20 Minutes | **Servings:** 4

Ingredients

- 1/(2) Seedless watermelons (cut into chunks)
- Lemon juice (freshly squeezed)

Method

Over the night freeze the watermelon chunks.

Place the frozen watermelon chunks and a tbsp of lemon juice into a blender and blend while occasionally adding lemon juice until smooth.

Serve and enjoy.

Nutritional Information

Cal: 86

Fat: 0g

Carbs: 22g

Fiber: 1g

Protein: 2g

Sugar: 18g

Dill Dip

This is an awesome blender recipe to include in your diet plan. Cheese is rich in calcium, it is an important ingredient for strong and prevention of tooth decay. It also contains sphingolipids and linoleic acid which is vital for cancer prevention.

Time: 26 seconds | **Servings:** 12

Ingredients

- 1 cup Greek yogurt (fat-free)
- 4oz. Neufchatel cheese
- 1/2 tbsp garlic powder
- 1/2 tbsp kosher salt
- 1tbsp dill (dried)
- 1/4 tbsp onion powder
- 1/2 tbsp parsley (dried)

Method

Add yogurt. Garlic powder, Neufchatel cheese, onion powder and salt to a blender (wildside+ jar) and blend.

Add parsley and dill then blend until blended completely.

Serve.

Nutritional Information

Calories: 35

Fat: 2g

Cholesterol: 5mg

Sodium: 135mg

Carbs: 1g

Fiber: 0g

Sugar: 0g

Protein: 3g

Butternut Squash Soup

This healthy and quick butternut squash soup is perfectly delicious with natural sweetness. A few steps with several Ingredients a smooth, flavorful bowl of soup is on the table. Butternut squash soup goes well with grilled cheese.

Time: 40 Minutes | **Servings:** 4

Ingredients

- 1 tbsp coconut oil
- 1 onion (diced)
- 1 butternut squash (peeled and cubed)
- 1 carrot (peeled and diced finely)
- 1 cubed green apple (peeled, cored)
- 3 Cups vegetable broth (low in sodium)
- 1 tbsp sea salt
- 1/4 tbsp ground ginger
- 1/4 tbsp curry powder
- 1/4 tbsp nutmeg (grated)
- 1/2 Coconut milk (canned)
- 1 tbsp sour cream (light)

Method

Heat oil in a Dutch oven. Add onion and cook until tender.

Add butternut, diced carrot, apple, and low sodium vegetable broth. Add salt ginger, curry powder, grated nutmeg.

Cook until the vegetables are tender.

Put the soup in a blender and blend. Mix in canned coconut milk.

Serve and enjoy when warm.

Nutritional Information

Cal: 161

Fat: 6g

Carbs: 27g

Fiber: 5g

Protein: 2g

Sugar: 10g

Conclusion

As you may notice, a blender is an essential, versatile kitchen appliance that can help you do so much more than making smoothies. It is a must-have equipment that allows you to mix up an array of Ingredients and blend them in Minutes to make a simple soup, margaritas, tapenade, casseroles, or any other yummy sauce.

This blender recipe book gives you easy blender recipes to try at home. It gives you a quick and fresh way to start your day, with only 30 blender recipes. However, there are a host of ways to use your blender. A blender gives you a lot of room to be creative. Explore blender recipes only and try to adjust or change the Ingredients to come up with delicious and easy-to-make blender recipes.

Author's Afterthoughts

THANK YOU

Thanks ever so much to each of my cherished readers for investing the time to read this book!

I know you could have picked from many other books, but you chose this one. So, a big thanks for downloading this book and reading all the way to the end.

If you enjoyed this book or received value from it, I'd like to ask you for a favor. Please take a few Minutes to post an honest and heartfelt review on Amazon.com. Your support does make a difference and helps to benefit other people.

Thanks for your Reviews!

Rachael Rayner

About the Author

Rachael Rayner

Are you tired of cooking the same types of dishes over and over again? As a mother of not one, but two sets of twins, preparing meals became very challenging, very early on. Not only was it difficult to get enough time in the kitchen to prepare anything other than fried eggs, but I was constantly trying to please 4 little hungry mouths under 5 years old. Of course I would not trade my angels for anything in the world, but I had just about given up on cooking, when I had a genius idea one afternoon while I was napping beside one of my sons. I am so happy and proud to tell you that since then, my kitchen has become my sanctuary and my children have become my helpers. I have transformed my meal preparation, my grocery shopping habits, and my cooking style. I am Racheal Rayner, and I am proud to tell you that I am no longer the boring mom sous-chef people avoid. I am the house in our neighborhood where every kid (and parent) wants to come for dinner.

I was raised Jewish in a very traditional household, and I was not allowed in the kitchen that much. My mother cooked the same recipes day in day out, and salt and pepper were probably the extent of the seasonings we were able to detect in the dishes she made. We did not even know any better until we moved out of the house. My husband, Frank is a foodie. I thought I was too, until I met him. I mean I love food, but who doesn't right? He revolutionized my knowledge about cooking. He used to take over in the kitchen, because after all, we were a modern couple and both of us worked full time jobs. He prepared chilies, soups, chicken casseroles—one more delicious than the last. When I got pregnant with my first set of twins and had to stay home on bed rest, I took over the kitchen and it was a disaster. I tried so hard to find the right ingredients and recipes to make the dishes taste something close to my husband's. However, I hated follow recipes. You don't tell a pregnant woman that her food tastes bad, so Frank and I reluctantly ate the dishes I prepared on week days. Fortunately, he was the weekend chef.

After the birth of my first set of twins, I was too busy to even attempt to cook. Sure, I prepared thousands of bottles of milk and purees, but Frank and I ended up eating take out 4 days out of 5. Then, no break for this mom, I gave birth to my second set of twins only 19 months later! I knew that now it was not just about Frank and I anymore, but it was about these little ones for whom I wanted to cook healthy meals, and I had to learn how to cook.

One afternoon in March, when I got up from that power nap with my boys, I had figured out what I needed to do to improve my cooking skills and stop torturing my family with my bland dishes. I had to let go of everything I had learned, tasted, or seen from my childhood and start over. I spent a week organizing my kitchen, and I equipped myself a new blender. I also got some fun shaped cookie cutters, a rolling pin, wooden spatulas, mixing bowls, fruit cutters, and plenty of plastic storage containers. I was ready.

My oldest twins, Isabella and Sophia are now teenagers, and love to cook with their Mom when they are not too busy talking on the phone. My youngest twins Erick and John, are now 10 years old and so helpful in the kitchen, especially when it's time to make cookies.

Let me start sharing my tips, recipes, and shopping suggestions with you ladies and gentlemen. I did not reinvent the wheel here but I did make my kitchen my own, started storing my favorite baking ingredients, and visiting the fresh produce market more often. I have mastered the principles of slow cooking and chopping veggies ahead of time. I have even embraced the involvement of my little ones in the kitchen with me.

I never want to hear you say that you are too busy to cook some delicious and healthy dishes, because BUSY, is my middle name.

Printed in Great Britain
by Amazon